Break Self: Feed

poems by

Gabrielle Myers

Finishing Line Press
Georgetown, Kentucky

Break Self: Feed

Copyright © 2024 by Gabrielle Myers
ISBN 979-8-88838-643-9 First Edition
All rights reserved under International and Pan-American Copyright Conventions. No part of this book may be reproduced in any manner whatsoever without written permission from the publisher, except in the case of brief quotations embodied in critical articles and reviews.

Publisher: Leah Huete de Maines
Editor: Christen Kincaid
Cover Art: *Redwood Forest* by Jill McLennan
Author Photo: Gabrielle Myers
Cover Design: Elizabeth Maines McCleavy

Order online: www.finishinglinepress.com
also available on amazon.com

Author inquiries and mail orders:
Finishing Line Press
PO Box 1626
Georgetown, Kentucky 40324
USA

Contents

We, the Makers 1
Why Die When You Can Change 2
Come this Way 3
Lover 4
Lover 5
Lover 6
We're There and Here 7
Begin 8
We Can't Stop 9
Break Self 10
"A Love Supreme," After Coltrane, After Harper 11
"Syeeda's Song Flute," After Coltrane, After Valentine ... 12
Alternate Version 13
Grow 14
Vessels 15
Bear 16
Distance 17
Tone of Voice 18
Los Amantes Saltan 19
"Life is uncertain as…" 20
Wither Each Stalk 21
Concoct 22
Warming and Us 23
With This Faith 24
"Syeeda's Song Flute," After Coltrane II 25
Smoke and Apples 26
Togetherness 27
Fire Ash 28
On the Delta Queen 29
Revision 30
After "Artichoke" by Edward Weston 31
After "Grass Against Sea," Edward Weston 32
Dunes 33
Reverse to Birth 34
A Song to Wholeness 35
The Bridge Walkers 36
Celebration of Ignorance 37
Riddle 38

Be in Lust with Life	39
We Are Not Rickety	40
Bare Offerings	41
Always Incipient	43
Expansion	44
"Invisible Germinations"	45
Break into Wholeness	46
Gentleness	47
Double Rapture	48
Song Makers	49
Spring Song: Swarm	50
Be a Person	51
Stillness's Lack	52
Reopening	53
Sight's Signals	54
Forward to Cradle	55
The Call	56
Gardening to Life the Organ	57
The Backside of the House	58
Super Moon Unmooring & Mooring	59
The Body's Mind Mending	60
"Confusion of Splendor"	61
Feathers Falling	63
Full Offering	64
The Cure	65
Spring Mostarda Making	66
Ode to Wild Mustard After Many Years of Drought	67
Atmospheric Rivers	68
Green Humming Earth	69
Never Rest in Dormancy Beyond the Proper Time	70
Symbol Shake	71
Flower Feeding	72
Bounty Set to Burst Forth	73
The Aftermath of Flourishing	74
Summer's Widening Aperture	75
The First Fire of Fire Season	76
Shadows on His Mind-Cave	77
You Can't Fly into a Mouth Filled with Past Fears of Burning	78
Everything We've Ever Loved Must End and Die and Reverse	79
Acknowledgments	81

"To keep becoming, always to stay involved in transition."
Arthur Miller

We, the Makers

No one has ever done us wrong.
   Losses ground into soil by our feet
      set to action. Don't cull seeds
         from lost love's leaf mat; pull
            down a ripening fruit, peel
               it open, and suck on new seeds,
                  birth them into being
                       with our waiting tongues' warmth.

Why Die When You Can Change

> *"Pray as though you were praying with someone else's soul."*
> —Charles Wright, "Body and Soul"

She should have lived as though living for someone else
Or tucked her sorrow and 'it misses the mark'
Into someone else's full mind leap into the moon.
She should have yearned for love's imperfections
And a cold isolation after giving her all,
Only to be brought to this place clear of all human
Distractions and attentions, where only she, too human,
Complicated her path.
She should have felt too much only to be hurt beyond
What she thought was repairable, to be wounded
To the fissures forming in her bones,
To be brought to herself in her cell-based presence,
To have to bring herself all whole again at age 41—
Bring herself into being, birthed five feet five,
With a mind thronging with decades of awareness
But no moments assembled, to have to pull
Memory fragments together again, round them whole,
Harness experiences that have no bottom feeling
Yet attached, mold them into what she wants them to mean.

Come this Way

Embrace interstices, divides,
sheer freedom rooted
in the self and not another,
shifting force's power in us
charged on another, another, another.

Lover

> *"Might I but moor—Tonight—On Thee!"*
> —Dickinson

After words
Spun through our salty mouths,
After bites of steak, tender,
And wine's tongue swim,
Let us break into ourselves—
Out of ourselves—
Through each other.

Lover

Wholly in
Each other
Aperture to aperture
Ride push ride push
Breath taken out
Take it
Given to me
A gift

Lover

What would it matter if we assigned
that other emotion
instead of lust, urge,
necessary action?

We take each other,
bare, deep,
as if we're tunneling
whole to the other
side of ourselves.

We're There and Here

> *"...because we are the branch, the iron blade, and sweet danger, ripening from within."*
> —R. M. Rilke

What if ripening took a mind-piercing blade,
a most romantic dream fulfilled
only to be emptied out, love
sowed into our heart and skin seams
only to be unraveled slowly enough
for us to sense each slip?
Too soft, feeling too much,
what did all of that get us?
Bruising's benefits don't
show on the surface, but inside
where our sweetness, our acidity
intensifies like a fig jam-bagged
by water-pulling sun's heat.

Begin

Doves have stopped coming to the neighbor's feeder.
The back neighbor's dog's sidewalk markings
have been wiped clean to the river.
                Sun makes growth happen
                behind valley fog; on the median strip,
                dried grasses push into greenness, change
                their essential selves back to growth.
Our minds return to beginning,
when the heart's plow pushed
into injuring, birthing sky.

We Can't Stop

Always the blooming out;
in our most desiccated and cold days,
              a resetting occurs, a waiting,
              a pull toward heat and baptism.
When something gets lost inside,
            when a hurt punctures
            passion's pressure,
we wait, we grow,
      slowly inch beyond skin's boundaries, beyond our husks,
steadily tent to another's warmth,
            burst to touch rough air,
pull ourselves into daylight's bareness.

Break Self

Run among leaf bloom, fruit plump, drop, rot—
all around us swells.
Decay's sweet, weighty scent
confused with blossom aroma.

This is where we have come, what we have made—
We've escaped to orange groves, palm trees,
places overflowing with flowers,
expanding greenness in February.
Run. Cycle through bloom, fruit, rot.
Feel fruit's stink waiting to expand,
push against former boundaries,
break itself.

"A Love Supreme," *After Coltrane, After Harper*

Concealed by our minds, our blood,
A pumping out, a release
Urged forth, unstoppable now.
Sweat on 102-degree days in swampland.
Water all around us, in us,
Leaking out, pushing out—
Out, out, urged forth—
Our supreme powers
Can't be contained, must spill forth,
Must coat us, drown us in our longing,
Our awareness, our ripening's stench—
His exhaustion spent, whole,
Born into this world, shaped, reshaped,
Not done yet.
Spill it out.
Get it out
From yourself,
Ourselves,
Yourself.

"Syeeda's Song Flute," *After Coltrane, After Valentine*

Almond petals unhinged
flood around grasses emerging through sidewalk cracks.
Fragrant rain lifts, dropping, lifts, dropping;
what will we make of us, here?
Uncharted, culling, culling, culling,
lifting ourselves, each other.
What will we make,
how will we make stop signs
merge into yellow yield, into green light?
Bounce, bounce, move—
there, here, there, don't stop;
we are the stop-time in the "center of constant movement,"
harness, grow, run the selves
onward, towards—

Alternate Version

Shift us, rupture us, bring us a full form.
    We can't hold too hard to old structures.
        Remake, bring ourselves whole
              like a green maple leaf shoots out,
                  glossy and smooth in its unfamiliar
                      path against rain-cleared air,
                          against fecund cow dung, car exhaust infiltrated air.
Each leaf cell born to unfurl a familiar structure,
      only to thrust a new version
              forward into bruising, coddling air.

Grow

March wind, breathing rain-packed
over saturated soil, over hanging grass tips,
ring in a beginning, let us forget
past dryness and death, spent fruit's harvest.
Let us be willing to wrestle with each other
in fields rising green; let us make ourselves
open against stinging thistle needles.

Blow through expanding leaf buds,
push them open and open,
until birth becomes our only option.
Ring out remnants of last year's loss;
usher in potential, bring it whole,
stuff it into our ears, our mouths.

Vessels

Curved flesh faces up to the sun,
catches what light gives,
reflects brightness and pollen
particles back to themselves.
Each turn and we flare,
ignite, spin off luminosity,
catch, hold, cast it back.
To hold and release, hold,
gather energy, release.
What energy that's out there is ours,
we, vessels of light.
We turn and turn electrons,
churn ourselves through each other
towards our own wholeness and dispersion versions.
Fill and cast back, spin brightness back upon itself
until no more shadow lingers,
everything in us and out
ignited, reborn
—our gift.

Bear

Double the intensity.
        Double the thrown down
                Inside outside pull.
To feel an us undulate inside,
        We've reinvented burned-out former lineaments,
                Redrawn boundaries that numbed and protected.
We hummingbirds birth as we withdraw,
        Set to bear ourselves and the other.

Distance

The city, soaked from days of rain, shifts water
through sycamores, through poplars, through the Seine.
Hemmed in humidity, our legs sticky with stasis,
we sit in cafes too long, stay
in front of paintings from long ago
too long to see their distance from us.
In the Vincennes, homeless camp;
their wood smoke wafts into honeysuckle and rose-infiltrated air—

To be somewhere, to go to where we never imagined;
to push a shoe into limestone crushed trails,
inhale with intoxication jasmine and croissant lined
city breaths, breathe in another possibility—
ah, we will have this,
only if we can see our way toward
another side of what we tend to think.

Tone of Voice

The same voices come
and dissipate to hold us,
swaddle only to release,
release into a train's rush
through vineyards, fields, mountains.
To hear the same voices
only to talk back now, to bend them
towards our benefit: control
hungers, ghosts' fixed voices.
Now that lonely child protected,
the outcast stands tall, overshadows
twelve-year old stairway tormentors,
the adult who forced her into a corner with his fists.
Bend our voice, pull in tunes to propel us,
be our voices' tuner.

Los Amantes Saltan

Shades grow upright,
Slide along the mountain rock face.
What lovers jumped, stupidly believing theirs the only love to have?
Let olive groves turn and turn into sunflower fields,
Let the towns stretch into city, city into country.
Devour thin fat as it curls on your tongue,
Eat a bristly artichoke heart, a liver fattened by force.
Don't think that if we're over we won't love again.

"Life is uncertain…" *

Life is uncertain.
Take me with you
Through searing city streets.
Make us one from two in woods by the river.
Bend yourself and me
To fit what we have in front of us:
Water smooth before dividing stones,
Cement cracks issuing from our boots,
Reasons to fall down beneath the sun.

* The title is a line by Apollinaire

Wither Each Stalk

Saturated spring, burn away
into summer's heat, wither each stalk which
grew, bent by moisture, towards light.
What we can, we take with us:
force peeling away
stutter of language and language;
a sweet lingering kiss, lip on lip;
a thought lifted, hung
by a palm leaf's tension.

Concoct

Dried sycamore leaves dusty with smoke ash
    won't hold our growth,
        that stirring of life pulses,
            works out a secret network beneath
                desiccated weeds and rotten lemons.
A process of increasing its reach,
    spreading wide over death and potential death—
        life is all around, saturating dry ground,
            harnessing fruits from hollow acorns, gestating seeds
                snapped by days over one hundred degrees.
Proliferation combs us with its tentacles—
    What will we make?

Warming and Us

For Brenda

Smoke spreads, steady microscopic particles
Rise and cling, we
Must do something we don't know how to do

Drying pine limbs, arms, fingers, their body parts
Crash and take down flimsy branches;
We must do something we don't know how to do.

Everyone who I wanted to believe
When I was younger told me that one voice
= a million. If we were
Smoke from the mountain fires,
We would rise, cling,
Blanket our parks and forests in a Safe Zone,
Buffer them from ourselves, our toxic spew.

But we're people tangled in our lives, our world;
We talk, write, take actions,
Sparingly so as to not let our energy
Evaporate too quickly, so as not
To spread ourselves bare for some cause and effect
We can't clearly point to
Even if we feel it like a seismic 8.0.

We must do something
We don't know how to do:
Make an Us up
From them, you, i.

With This Faith

Particles rise and fall, caught
        In thick sunlight bands projecting from the window.
Make up belief. Lead
        With faith in evolution.
Particles in sunlight rise and float, suspended;
        In a semi-dark room, we might not see them as separate.
What makes tiny objects fly around in a sunlight dance
        Is our belief, our dramatization of their existence;
They mean we're not fixed, should feel each other's
        Reformation and rebirth.
Make up belief, feel flighted, grow again
        Into what we might be meant to be.
Trust belief
        Until it aligns what we see.

"Syeeda's Song Flute," *After Coltrane* II

With this faith:
A free air fall catches
Us whole.
Hot pins of cold rain
Pronounce what gives life:
Hot head cooled by pins.
Concoct: merge, merge, merge;
Our dust and clods from turned soil
Flake from us, release beyond you and me,
Become a beyond us
Into a we that thinks beyond.

Smoke and Apples

Apples never left to rot
made into cider, sweet fritters.
Autumn sun and blue air crisped in coolness.
In the valley, smoke hovers 1,053 feet in height,
but here air tickles our lungs with clarity;
we can see light glint, a pond's surface slickness.
What people have made: 11 days of hazardous air;
11 days of fire burning forest and forest and home and business;
11 days of people burning and running from flames.
What distance we have created from our destruction,
what contrast: our kisses and deep tunneling creation,
sipping wine, talking, watching light
slip beneath flare-red amber leaves.

Togetherness

We were meant to see us
in all our agony:
our bodies twisted up,
buoyant lift towards the other realm,
weightless turning, awareness
of what had been untouched by us inside;
the pull down to our basic instincts—
a lashing out, out, out at each other,
the one who dared take us to that lucid realm,
only to bring us crashing back towards
the one filled with others' traffic,
not enough money's constant noise.
Our pride congests us;
we were taken up so high
only to be brought back.

Fire Ash

The Camp Fire's smoke eases into spaces
between oak leaves, its particulate matter dispersed
into lungs, into summer, into seven-month dried grass blades.
What we can breathe, we breathe.

What we can think our way out of,
we do and then think toward an us
outside of matter's weight and pressure,
out of smoke's cool valley blanket
which chills us more than Tule Fog's hold.

The dog park, empty of dogs,
sits like a blank beach waiting for waves
that will not come. Dryness
has cemented sidewalk spaces;
dirt cracks with lines
fine as an Orb Weaver's web. Dead
Crabgrass clings to torn hamburger wrappers.

Feel an Us apart from what
we thought ourselves toward
slip out, unleash self, unhinge
from soil that has abandoned us;
leap us up past the inversion layer
into the giving air next week's rains will bring,
into greenness' incipient cascade.

An Us will envelope the valley,
create streams and rivers again from here to the Delta,
scrape out with its thick, bushy roots any
doubt, any plaque that has accumulated
in the tangled veins leading to our
pumping, life
-giving muscle.

On the Delta Queen

Overlooking the Sacramento River After Its Convergence with the American River

The tourist train blows its horn,
makes its steam pushing effort known.
Motorboat wake creates white crests
that crash against old bridge pilings.
Dry sun ignores shade cloth.
Agricultural runoff and river life and bugs
we cannot see rush past, steady in their intent
to meet the Delta's marshes,
set in their path to the Pacific, their freedom
from land, their joining with water
and more water, until their water is lost,
given to a whole, made less their own.
Sometimes we know we can be like this;
ourselves given up to an us, to preserve
ourselves we flow into one another
until what one brings doesn't matter.

Revision

Sing a tune to another narrative
of us, me, you.
    Each time we reach for each other,
    we should be hummingbirds shocked
    in their rise to a pomegranate's open flower.
        Each time we turn away, we should grasp
        to one another as if the cliff below
        held a heated bed that we could wrap
        all of our problems in, to forget, but not confront.
            Forget that which turns and turns;
            leave those barren hollow bones
            to decompose in what is yet to come.

After "Artichoke," by Edward Weston

Rub through tough, finger-resistant leaves,
feel into creases that separate center
from what protects it. Dig down through layers
to fine hairs that lift away—
don't let oxygen and harsh air particles
turn that nucleus soft,
discolor it in the falling evening light;
sprinkle preserving acidic juice to keep it fresh,
protected, untarnished. Hold
that core apart, then peel back into it
until exposed and ready to take on
steam, grill grates, boiling water,
a hot sear to make it whole for our tongues.

After "Grass Against Sea," Edward Weston

In our minds we retreat back to the edge,
comfort ourselves in end of land sadness,
rest in the lines of cypress that delineate
one field from the next; the hill rise and its crest
as it divides this from that, the clear cut
before land rips away from ocean,
grass spears rise against swollen seas.
Let us bask in the spears' tips that push
and stab into fog lifted air: fine points
exist, fine points puncture one realm from another,
move in the ocean's pull away from land.
Preserve edges, celebrate their distinct
boundaries; let the wind rustle and stop,
shake and stop, throttle only to pause and spread.

Dunes

The dryness could go on forever,
it could fold and rise, extend beyond
what we see today, what we hope for tomorrow.
The emptiness and craving could be there,
pull us long into next year,
stretch themselves beyond the decade, the century.
We could remain isolate,
we could stop ourselves
from extension, from commingling,
from growing out to another to become
more than this
one.

Reverse to Birth

An offering we each have
something to pull down
move through ourselves to another
we each have little eggs
waiting in our bellies
oh to make it up, believe it
to throw ourselves into thick longing
our beginning plasma
let the butterflies that block us
be turned back into cocoons and fibers
of what is yet to be, reversed to birth again

A Song to Wholeness

Lake water/ still mountains/
fine birch leaves/ snow lines mirrored:
let us mirror this placidity, a sureness.
Let us mirror this dip, dip;
no longer pieces of one body—
wholeness lies in what we find,
not in the self, that timeless lie,
we seek for a reason.
Dip, turn, hold, release,
stop searching for another beyond us;
let sureness bring us back, motion sureness back.
Mirror a motion to kiss, lick love.
Make an us up
out of mountain stillness, water tension, golden leaf quiver,
out of a cool sky's starkness
warming into itself, waking open.
Blow on our stillness to let us rise
whole, together, joined
stronger from fracture,
from leaving our former selves.
Hold an us; move, move,
go toward it, hold it, hold
—quiver searching for an us—
vibrate higher
in sureness, in release,
in go, in motion back,
in motion towards,
in motion towards yourself as whole;
whole we are as one
though fully functioning before,
though moving through ice caps,
forests, sweating before—
higher, higher, get higher
until we explode, join,
lose, merge, one from two:
whole.

The Bridge Walkers

After Adrienne Rich

The wires on the bridge could cut us to shreds,
but they mean to hold us up,
buoyant toward winter's light glare,
cradle us to the next phase of place—
to work, home, back through bright air's cage.
Like swallows we move through wire,
pass a subway tunnel's steaming vents,
pass what we might become
if we linger too long. Each day's
light stream forces us to walk
into a day's next variation,
forces us forward into each other,
bound by light's air, uncaged,
humming like wires set in motion
to open, bridge our narratives.

Celebration of Ignorance

We can't see inside the dove's head,
but a some thing
shifts us to wake.
Awaken, come to an elms' serrate leaves
swirl against sycamores' broad edges,
hear dove wings tremble toward fence
only to collapse against her own frame,
smell wisteria blooms,
car exhaust, chicken-infused fryer oil
crest on the wind's wings and move toward us.
Each day we look at ourselves,
each day we turn toward skin,
nail, twist of bones,
let us snap in alertness,
realize we know nothing about ourselves or another,
start again from nothingness
to forge, hone, contrive
from no firm place, no understanding
of where we are or who.

Riddle

Hem in all parts
Of us that ring disparate.
Pull all shards back
In stop time to their center
Joining. Thread, stitch,
Weave another, firmer
Genesis. If we're here,
If we're cast out,
Let us spin back to a root,
Crown ourselves' new construction queen,
Build a throne around our incipience,
Take a leaking heart to our hearth,
Coddle it back to seal itself whole.

Be in Lust with Life

What part of us lingers, lunges like a fevered bat
into a pepper plant's shade as it unfurls verdant leaves?
Fence planks protect us,
pull us toward ourselves
in unseen, unchartered ways.
Keep a piece of ourselves
that is a self to ourselves
—let it out, but never hold it
out like a smacked palm.

If necessary, retain who we are.
We can always retreat into our stoic parts,
release back to a previous shape,
reform, resilient as dough
worked by tough hands.
We have been worked by decades
of gain and loss, hard work, meager wages, long hours,
creating to be in lust with life, with existence,
with rain's kiss and sun's benediction.

We Are Not Rickety,

despite the worry.
We gleam and alight,
unwinged yet set to sing,
set to usher forth others
into song, dance, sacred hum
—that same hum that bees make
as they gather close to blossom mouths,
open and ready to give, to get.
We rise: watch our luminous climb.

We glide down close to soil,
watch worms wiggle and know
they move in unison with us,
match our motion and the bees' motion.
Worms shimmy and even their shit is gold;
even when they get cut in half, they grow
to be more than one—they divide, conquer.

We will sing out.
We will make leaves throb
with brilliant realization, quicken
with awareness of what is yet to come.
What fruits we will make together
—our cornucopia will unfurl as the sun
makes her way toward us, as the moon
ignites our slumber and leap to reap.

Bare Offerings

I.
By our own minds
        we collapsed inward, shut down
                all feeding electrical waves.
We let our eyes cut off any
        glimpse of a life beyond
                what rested before our eyes.
As if we knew that we would feel
        too much or too little for that other.
As if we knew that a puttering out
            was much worse than a dramatic explosion,
                    worse than facing ourselves and our own
                            narratives of loss, worse than letting go
                                in a way that punctured.

II.
By our own hands, we let our minds
        collapse inward, shut down
                all feeding electrical waves.
We let our eyes cut off any
        glimpse of a life beyond
                what rested before our eyes.
In a head contained, did we feel safe?
        In a body untouched, feed by the familiar,
                would we not yearn for escape through another?
How would we be able to hold
        bone, skin, blister, nail, hair,
                wanting to be whole?

III.
We let our eyes cut off any
        glimpse of a life beyond
                what rested before our eyes.
We turned away from illumination,
            coveted our ignorance of what could
                be changed by us. We deferred
                significance for another time, an unknown place,

other versions of ourselves, other ways
        of erecting and launching our translucent,
                            bare offerings.

Always Incipient

We grow again like a plant cut to dividing points
flushes out verdant leaves, catches spring light.
We move, take air, take
nourishment from unseen places.
What urge pushes us to extend long into days,
chase ourselves' future revisions,
pretend stasis never happens:
we always feel compelled to go, run,
leap over losses, set to pull up
to our being's next level, our next sustaining meal.
Let our coming fruit
bear forth splendors
we couldn't have imagined
before knowing the other.

Expansion

While we sleep, tubers root beneath our bed.
Our sheets become large limbs arcing into wood floor;
our arms lengthen into year-old roots that push
us against each other, against mattress.
Lupine sprout from our eyes; bees emerge
from our lips; in our ears, crickets sing,
etch still air with an incessant song.
Sheets turn into loam, our feet dip
into a small pond fecund
with tadpoles growing into frogs—
frogs that with their peeps usher forth spring.
Our fingers touch, we fuse with mycelium networks,
spores launch from our nails,
ring in our evolution's new tale.

"Invisible Germinations"

Networks map beneath our feet;
energy nodules pulse and press messages
to our toes to fruiting mushroom bodies to a lemon tree's
knobby roots. In the sky, synapses
send messages from star to moon to earth to star;
undulations communicate our germination,
our thrust onward together.
Together with the lemon and mushroom,
we move through electrical impulses.
We throb with an urge to be,
mass, accumulate, spread growth.
Seeds break hull surface,
vibrate and dance in soil
—our feet lift.

Break into Wholeness

In fracture, light enters spaces
left from our cleavage; through separation
something stronger spreads out,
a firmer cement seeps into our cracks.
We rupture ourselves, suffer
a division from what kept us whole,
capture a new light we couldn't see,
let it enter our most sacred spaces,
saturate, transfigure our base selves.

Gentleness

After Anne Dufourmantelle

A double gift makes us a home among our prior destruction.
Crumble the structure's remnants that we couldn't hold;
let jagged pieces implode on themselves.

Let us bring ourselves together in loss
of what would not work, of what failed
to make us gentle toward each other.

Double Rapture

Unmappable, this night space
that surrounds us, contains us
in countershot to what we've said
on our worst days. Wager on what
can't be named; relay meanings'
after glow, its intention.
Get to before ritual,
before lines were drawn for us, between us.
Let's find a detour that reroutes us
to a new feeling and thinking landscape,
takes us to before division, to a double rapture,
a taking in of rain drops
which tremble against window glass
as our dancing boots shake walls.

Song Makers

What makes us bend down to listen,
turn toward each other's vibration,
as if swarming not away from ourselves
but inward and outward, equipoised
to become hearers of what the other mouth
needs to sing?

Rhythmical in our dips in and out,
our songs ringing bells that awaken,
entreat others to bend toward another's pitch.

Spring Song: Swarm

After Rilke

Be bees quick to dive into flower heads
as if behind us rest wind and desiccating dryness.
For we can intone a way of listening, of hearing
that, when other voices stop, we are left with mouths.

Be those who plunge into dancing throngs;
climb the ladder and let our bodies move down among hands.
Here, do not let any hurt or move away lessen our propulsion—
be ones who forever sing of coupling, union.

Be disparate, not bendable toward scorn or isolation.
Be voices that ring into another and another
so that in our hearing we return to ourselves.

Join in the interchange that fuels and lifts,
stocks up only to yield and yield for others—
add ourselves to the swarm and fill the world with fruit.

Be a Person

From emergence's wetness,
we peel back faith veils,
learn boundaries that create one,
study others' circumferences,
study who they be, who we be.
Intent on defining ourselves as people,
personality, 'this is me!' 'this is me!'
murky waters tumble into our brains—
with each layer we pull,
turn out.

Stillness's Lack

Stillness we lack,
        nosedive into each movement,
                      turn, turn, fluid like pigeons
taken from a barn, left forty-seven miles northwest,
        always finding our way
                back to plunge into our barn's open doors,
                      leave their frames loose.
What part of ourselves we thought
        abandoned, we return to on each dip,
                feel movement's familiarity,
                      wind's flight echo, air's hollowness
speak to how one motion
        never usurps another, but goes
                straight for our mind's mending.

Reopening

Walk among plywood boarded shop windows,
office buildings left empty, a year's dark panes,
discarded face masks gathered near drainage grates.
In front yards, oxalis's yellow cups open to our voices,
tulips unwind in fragile March light,
roses pruned of old growth
begin a shiny unfolding, a stubborn climb.
Under highways, the homeless, tent-gathered,
pass on worn sneaker feet those in car comfort.

We each make our way out,
again in motion,
again reach for another,
again pull ourselves forward
from retreat, from house-honed minds.
What possibilities will we feel
as residues of our thinking?
What will echo inside us
as we walk beneath immense leaves,
plum petals catch in our hair,
butterfly wings cull our tongues to speak?

Sight's Signals

See oxalis's yellow newness
open to plum blossom shadow.
See the calf, nose to hayfield,
inhale growth's still warm aroma.
See an old man emerge from his house den,
his ridged eyelids open to our Delta's swift breeze.
Wind pulls through palm frond,
through amber's bursting leaf trail.
Whatever need we have to savor
our losses' remnants,
to fix our minds on shriveled promises,
let us thwart ourselves,
so that our opening strikes us
right through our spines,
ignites our synapses,
awakens us to sight's signals.

Forward to Cradle

Wind pushes like a force from inside
Brought out to make us remember:
We must move forward into our beyond
Without promise's tight grip that we held for years.
Make up how to cherish a cactus flower's spiraling openness.
Make up how to meld flavor's tang in lemon, honey, fermented peppers.
Make up how to ease ourselves
Into our rhythmic syllables as Pacific waves tumble
Against Santa Monica cliffs, bring sand into their folding.
Make up a forgetting of his imprint, his ushering forth feeling.
Never forget our energy spinning in and out of our mouths, our fingers,
Our arms leaning forward to cradle what we cannot yet imagine.

The Call

Tuned, pitched toward touch,
its miniscule vibrations set for reception,
we catch notes, become speakers
who spin back incantations, cast all back.
What railings we ride out of numbness,
what bars we slide down sure in our thrust
toward a wave's bending coolness and scattering.

We won't let our pain tell our narrative,
won't seal ourselves in like puppets in tin boxes.
We hold what dense air we can,
spring forward, free ourselves
from thought bars into sirens,
reimagine fingers, ears,
tongues that tickle themselves
to rip through speech.

Gardening to Life the Organ

Our self caught inside the San Marzano's first tomato,
We cling to ribs that line each side, each ventricle tears
As we dip to the seeds.
Our pumping muscle shakes thin flesh walls,
Tries to ignite sweetness and acidity's trap
That closes in on one fruit.

Our hope dug in our garden's soil,
Each worm wiggles and tunnels into vessel walls,
Each half-decomposed orange rind smears
Against love's hope edge, love's impossible decline.
The Calabrian pepper's roots web out,
Fuel a thin trickle
Thumping from the worn organ
As it bleeds into sand grains,
Into twigs set to nourish in dissolution
As it gives to nematodes, to basil sprouts.

The Backside of the House

Water cycles through our aquaculture system.
Thousands of small rocks catch and filter fish poop,
turn it into fuel for a three-year old Purple Hungarian Pepper
crowding out New Zealand Spinach's creep.
A mantis's hard eggshell grips a tomato's pliable stem,
sets itself on birth and birth.
When we sit still above the worm bin,
we can hear their slick bodies
slither in carrot peel and torn lettuce.
Even butterflies have returned
to their jagged flights near the fig.
Everything grows forward, everything
around us turns out another interpretation of itself.
We can spin other narratives of us,
leave first stems severed to the compost's rot,
mend into broader, more spacious leaves
set to catch more light.

Super Moon Unmooring & Mooring

Apex to apex we move, vibrate, lift higher.
What essence of me,
what root of you
gets thrown out from our bodies in the cabin's still air?
What histories and perceptions
will pitch themselves into new imaginings
as we move forward through unchartered
territories within ourselves?

Electrified, plugged into our feedback loops,
connected to synapses in each other's bodies
as if cresting on a wave that could bring us up to the super moon,
never place us inside human bodies in a limited way,
limitless now,
like white caps that rise to disappear
to rise, ride, join, push in, meet,
go forward into each other.

The Body's Mind Mending

Moon's bright cast thickens pine needles,
pushes out the dirt road,
widens thistle flowers
just opened for the day's bloom.
Out the bedroom window,
gaps between grasses and rocks close.

What stories we've told ourselves now appear
false, what distances we tried
to etch with our minds
dissolve in our bodies' need
to smell compost's decomposition, mycelium's spread,
to hear a hummingbird's vibrating wings in hemlock ascension,
to touch our skin's warmth, feel it pull us back
into our bodies, their perfect soils set for extension.

Wideness opens us into each other, into fields
pulsing with cricket chorus and tunneling worms.
Whatever hold has us, let it release us
into more awe at what these bodies are capable of,
what they can teach our minds.

"Confusion of Splendor"

After Neruda

I.
Through plum petal and discarded mask confusion,
through days filled with screen stare and wind
tearing limb from tree home, we make our way forward.
Our first numbness melts into accentuated touch,
each nerve pricked towards full embrace
of what it can sense. Each note our ears
catch and pull toward their drums
reverberates forever in our hearing, imprinted into our minds'
meaning landscapes like a canyon pressed into being
by the river's ever flowing mountain motion force.
We become less of what we were, more of what
we thought we could be, let go of false images,
fictions we developed in response to others' fictions,
move into our cells as they are, mutating, reshaping,
coded with memories of joining, whole.

> II.
> Divided into lips and ears,
> we take speech, taste its syllables,
> let them roll around and out towards
> muted arrows and buried hatchets.
> Let our tongues' violence
> turn to tones eased for hearing.
> We gave ourselves to the thistle's
> seed spread promise, to dispersion.
> We bent our lobes to listen
> for stirrings speaking through forest mulch,
> pollen-coated walls issuing notes from beehives.
> All of the words we spoke, what good have
> they done for our hearing?

>> III.
>> Our hearts oiled like an olive's inner flesh,
>> we dive in, perpetual in forward motion.
>> Our threads unbound, pull, reaffix
>> to skin, eye, finger, nose.

What hardness rests in our hearing?
What stones have never
congested our dreams of joining?
We, aligned with the hummingbird's
precision in pulling out sustenance,
leap into another's red flower,
let fullness's fragrance fill us,
hurl us through the air to join,
never be separate, never be just one.

Feathers Falling

Dragonflies steady themselves above tilled grasses,
Dive to nudge their noses in soil clod's coolness.
Our hummingbird, the one we see every morning,
Dips down to eye-level—wing hum, eye lock, accelerated rise.

Our wells run dry in the mountains;
Neighbors pull water for weed grows, wine grapes.

Springs' trickles feed
Blackberry thickets and watercress which shrink to fit
August's drip. In the valley, smoke
Nestles rice tips, coddles a playground's seesaw.

We make our way through dryness, smoke, unknowns,
Know we will leap toward one another, cast fecundity out.

Our minds can't hold our gifts in, can't hold our force—
We give not to get, transform our destruction illusion.

Our eyes, bees that race to rub pollen between their lashes.
Our fingers, hummingbirds' beaks that rise to flower columns.
Our toes, hermit crabs scuttling across beaches,
Finding safe pockets in volcanic rock.
Our hair threads, spiders' webs attaching to plum branches
Firm enough for holding.

Full Offering

Locked forehead to forehead, we sip
Each other in, dig to find what was not lost,
What cannot be erased or pushed away.
Grasshoppers spin in star-thistle patches.
Sheep chomp on spiky seed heads.
Two hummingbirds rise
One hundred and three feet above
Sweet peas now rid of flowers, now casting out pods.

Our ribs expand to pull in smoked air.
Fires burn to our east, to our north, green trees
Turn to kindling, towns fuel blazes, sustain ignition.

The land around us once charred, glass melted, trees
Became black skeletons reaching out in mountain air.

Now grasses return, now woodpeckers
Thrive as they nestle acorns in pine trees,
Now new seedlings emerge, now
New thoughts begin to fill spaces
Between trees fallen and surviving through burn.

Everything's task begins with destruction's reframing,
Drips like our sweat into parched earth,
Turns the desiccated over on itself enough
That germination infuses every crevice;
What gets ignited grows into something
Pressurized, torn, hurt, reunified
Into its full offering.

The Cure

Onion seedlings begin their fragile lift.
Thin shoots raise, timid in their growth
Under dry fall's brief rain cast.
We can't be hesitant anymore, must pull
Ourselves forward with firmness
Regardless of who stands with us or retreats,
Regardless of rain's pound or absence.

Create drops from dry clouds.
Etch growth pathways through leaf litter,
Through caustic smoky winds, through ash.
Grow profound in our movement up.
Ascend into late fall's thinning light.
Lilt as we climb, lift,
Linger in air's curing emptiness.

Spring Mostarda Making

Spill yellow seeds like loose marbles to toast against hot steel,
                      send them to swell in plum juice,
                                  expand with balsamic's sweet acid
condensed by summer's sun, by light filtered through smoke
                                      —ignite spice,   tang, tingle.
    Sense how firm greenness softened
                            to purple on weighted stems.
Our orchards' branches curled in drought's evaporative pull,
our wells emptied themselves to keep us full,
our apricots, plums, figs wrinkled under
                            heat's weight, under drought's pressure point.
Now our trees' buds tumefy, tent out broad leaves,
   flower after flower unfolds to rain rivers,
        roots expand beyond our seasonal streams,
            reach out and down for sustenance,
                ready to rise above coming desiccation.
Savor each season's water concentration,
                          lick each year's deluge, taste mustard's pop, its thrust.
Swirl sweet plum sacks, vinegar's sharp clearing,
oil's cure rounding us—a filling.

Ode to Wild Mustard After Many Years of Drought

Its budding brings fields and rows flush with yellow unfolding,
                                                  each petal opens out, erects
above expanding greenness,
                escalates above dry season's parched patches.
Our seasonal streams once filled with hot rocks, withered grasses, spent
                      seed heads, our wells ran to empty taps in the foothills,
                                    our forests fired on, furious to find ignition.
Now atmospheric rain rivers funnel water
                      into its growing cells, push out blossoms.
Undeterred by our narratives of destruction,
                          it advances, brings seeds into our holding,
                          soon to fill our mouths with tang, piquancy,
                          soon to fuel blood thumping through our veins,
                          soon to not let us fall at our own hands,
                          soon to show us what we've done
                                  —how could we forget how
                                          it self-sows, roots down, rises for us to reap.

Atmospheric Rivers

Leave the house ready to throw ourselves
into yellowing leaf and greening grass hesitation,
life's throng in rainy season's first thrust.
Let our minds spill out beginnings from each end.
Let yesterday's dry dirt lift with 1,001 seedlings,
their fuzzy tips not deterred by last night's chill.
Let what threatens to kill us rise
like a bulb's head through our hearts,
allow us to grip to another variation as the dark
head gives way to broad leaf expansion.
Whatever thoughts we had about ending, about giving way
to smoke and desiccation, have been given wings
to fly headfirst into rain's atmospheric river.
Drops never end in our minds, never dissipate
from our vein's springs; liquid falls all around
—let it raise us to our blessing.

Green Humming Earth

Lady bugs' pin-like bodies pulse.
Hear the frogs' moaning chins
Hit mud, send signals to shake pond walls.
Wild golden lilies throw petals open.
The ceanothus' tails cast pollen on lily lips,
Fall soft against their tongues.
In the field lupine gather against hill rise;
Their perfect bells build to our breaths,
Spring into their scents. Fall against
A charred pine limb. Watch the green sprouts
Push from the burn. What we take forward:
Nymphs gathering to dance at sunset,
Thousands of baby dragonflies rise
Forward into fecund amber light,
Double-wings lost in their potential, vibrating against
The edges of each other's wings.

Never Rest in Dormancy Beyond the Proper Time

Let lupine stuff our noses with spring's
level light. What blocked us, let it spill
out into our pasture thick with vetch.
Proliferation profits from the groundhog's earth pockets,
tunnels extend long into our garden,
throw digested earth on the gravel road.
A burned pine fell across the upper pasture in last night's storm.
Another charred oak crashed down three
Manzanita on the fire road. Last night needling hail
hit the fig's new growth, ricocheted into switchgrass.
Now cypress seedlings reach through freezing air's
sudden burst which interrupted spring's
increasing heat and light progression.
The stormy chill set us in stop time between two seasons,
silenced the peeper frog chorus and forest nymphs'
ethereal rise. What inevitable resurgence
of mayfly, star thistle, and blackberry do we count on?
What "never rest in dormancy beyond the proper time"
do we hold in our human bellies,
our internal clocks scratching out chants
to a summer afternoon's black bird chorus?

Symbol Shake

Countless tiny petals from thousands
of small flowers undulate in wind.
With a flutter, with a flip,
fragrance fills us with allure.
What will we take home in the cold season,
wisps of a frozen breeze encasing us in hibernation?
Seeds that didn't blossom last year do this year.
If the city we used to roam in is too far away now
for us to imagine our former walks down sycamore lined streets
—chip bags, crashed bottles, cigarette butts gathering against curbs—
what does that say about our memories,
our holding, our ability to pull
our past close in our minds, to keep it in mind,
covet our former selves as symbols of what might become?

Flower Feeding

Under the May moon's growing light,
lupine unfurl their tight stacked blossoms,
baby kittens make their way out from beneath storage sheds,
Mayflies rise against a brisk sun set.
What are we meant to do,
but plant seeds into thawing, drying soil?
What are we meant to do,
but hold each other up to cumulous clouds,
to hail that pounds against flesh,
to the opening a hummingbird gives
after its flower feeding?

Bounty Set to Burst Forth

       Tiny toads jump between our fingers as we pull lambs quarters and thistle from garden beds. In front of us, burned pines, sentinels of our rebirth, reach their jagged tops towards clear sky. We've walked the canyon slope past hundreds of dead trees, looked up to their charred bodies, dried limbs, hoping one doesn't fall on us and knock us out on the fire road. This morning, so many birds whose names we don't know sung in unison at the day's warming. Our mustard plants which gave us 11 rounds of harvest now go to seed, green pods fatten in June's heat; the leaves toughen, ready to be turned to mulch. What proliferation did we turn from before, ignorant of the potential surrounding us, not sensing our bounty set to burst forth?

The Aftermath of Flourishing

Solstice sun rises, pushes out dew's lingering moisture from grass seeds.
Once purple and white variegated flowers now grow into prickly star-like
Heads that dig into our socks and ankles, cling to dog fur and sheep hide.
The momma toad who birthed her babies in our garden
Has retreated to our spring.
When we water the tomatillos, tomatoes, and basil, baby toad after baby toad
Hops across raised beds, seeking cover in the garden's safe edge.

What started to move into wholeness before has been met with the aftermath
Of its flourishing; what died last year has been rebirthed from seed, attended
With rain and our watering can, endured the early summer's heat rise
To just below 99 F.
What knowledge can we harness in our bones, push out like the sun pushes
Dew from thinning straw blades?
What lessons in care can we extract from the seed hull
Which nourishes for months and months?
What will the mamma toad speak with her deep-throated horn, her call
Widening out from our spring, filling the canyon in her urging
For us to raise ourselves whole?

Summer's Widening Aperture

Nematodes and microbials eat through seemingly dry soil,
plow through surface desiccation to extract a buffet,
feed on forgotten roots and pine bark fragments.

Summer's heat pumps into our toes and fingers.
Amassing pressure builds to release in a tomato's stem.
An electric pull moves us down hills towards a creek's edge.
A world's widening aperture forces us to wake
to water's movement over smooth rocks,
water's push through drying mountains,
its underground, inevitable cascade towards us.

The First Fire of Fire Season

Smoke blows in its charge
led by cumulous ignition explosions.
Grasses once swimming in lupine fields
have dried to brittle seed heads
snapping in afternoon's hot breeze.

Down canyon near the spring,
toads birthed in our garden weeks ago
gather, wet their skins with the high Sierra's snowmelt
filtered through miles of shale and granite.

What fireworks did we throw into our campfires,
so intent on maintaining tradition despite potential devastation?
What flares will we throw into crowds that contain our children,
the throngs where we used to dance,
the garden plots where we would gather with our grandparents?
Our oak tree's leaves now coated in ash's thin layer;
Our strawberry pots litter with burned brush particles.

What water we can harness,
we do. What tanks we should have filled;
what ponds we should have dug;
what swales we should have made around our ranches;
what rivers we should have partially dammed.

Our children will hide on creek banks,
bury themselves in blackberry thickets on spring's
edges, hold clammy toad skin
to press knowledge into our human veins,
to think our way to a new level of licking,
of absorbing vibrating earth, pulsing spring,
burning trees left like shadows on our hillsides
still growing from their bases out.

Shadows on His Mind-Cave

Tequila, ale, weed-tar scented breath;
gashed knuckles once open in tender holding;
cyan-blue eyes littered with red webs.
Turn your erupting hate upon me.
Rip me with dumbass and idiot,
words like hot spit frothing from a mouth
which hours earlier said love you, see you soon.
Precious water which belongs to our seedlings
spent in an upward lift to my face,
spent directing rage at something outside of yourself.
What volcanos spew lava on your mind?
What betrayals devour your potential at stability?
What misassigned anger do you laud on our love?
What traps has your past set against your future?
Take the pillow and throw it at me.
Take the plastic bottles once filled with fertilizer for our tomatoes,
and pitch them at the hope of an us.
Take the shadows which dance against your mind-cave,
hurl them into the forest fire rising in a near canyon.
Let the burning rid you of the haunting of an us,
of the almost freedom that whispered in your bent ears.

You Can't Fly into a Mouth Filled with Past Fears of Burning

Let dust rise thirteen feet high behind our car wheels.
Let withered lupine give their seeds to dry soil.
Let red worms spin down to find moisture near the fig's roots.
Let fires that rage to our north and south burn all remnants of hope.
Let hope's attachment release and float pine trees' incinerated bodies forward.
Let what we tried to mold with our calloused hands
crumble against our tongues.
What we tried to erect out of ashes, out of a spring's trickle,
couldn't sing with two hands, couldn't fly
into a mouth filled with past fears of burning,
into a mind clogged with memories of loss.
Watercress builds and gathers near a spring's outlet;
blackberry vines grow unimpeded near a lake's lips.
Let our promise move from a joining to a centering,
a thrusting out from our powered center.
Let our mind set on becoming more than one
turn inward to clip any division,
reform and align what we envision
with what will grow from our fields
that pop with lilting grasshoppers,
splitting seed heads, shattering pinecones.

Everything We've Ever Loved Must End and Die and Reverse

Ceanothus, pine, and manzanita smoke plumes
lift from our canyons, rise above our rivers,
pull their particulates toward dispersion,
spread over our pastures, slink
stealthily states away. Our forests' fragments
head out from their genesis, leave their essences
burned to their roots burrowing deep in red soil.
Born to change states, born to grow and rise,
charr and leave to another place, form, mass.

Find symmetry in our diffusion, our shape-shift
to manage ourselves. Find promise in destruction,
in a pine needle's flare. Along burned-out trunks
termites thrive in thousands of tunnels,
snakes and groundhogs burrow and dig down,
flanked in cover. Everything we've ever loved
must end and die and reverse; everything
we've ever wanted to hold onto will wrestle
itself free from any hold. Find solace in transition,
in endings—turn them into beginnings
set open for fields of acorns
to break into being.

Acknowledgments

Catamaran, Fall 2020, "After 'Grass Against Sea,' Edward Weston"

Edible East Bay, Spring 2022, "Spring Mostarda Making" and "Ode to Wild Mustard After Many Years of Drought"

Koan: Paragpon Press, Summer 2018, "We're There and Here" and "Lovers, I"

pacificREVIEW: A West Coast Art Review Annual, Spring 2020, "Vessels" and "Los Amantes Saltan"

Thank you to Leah Maines and the *Finishing Line Press* team for believing in my work.

Thank you to my writing mentors who are alive and long dead, who I've known in person and only through their writing: Brenda Hillman, Rusty Morrison, Laura Walker, Pam Houston, Sharon Olds, Matthew Zapruder, Brian Turner, Marilyn Abildskov, Allan Williamson, Sandra McPherson, Juan Felipe Herrera, Claudia Rankine, Bob Hass, Joe Wenderoth, Joy Harjo, Joshua Clover, Rhoda Trooboff, Craig Santos Perez, James Baldwin, Wesley Gibson, Audre Lorde, Graham Foust, Michelle Bitting, Anna Akhmatova, Michael Harper, Marilyn Chin, Louise Erdrich, Rainer Maria Rilke, Giuseppe Ungaretti, Brian Teare, Robert Creeley, Pablo Neruda, Fernando Pessoa, Etheridge Knight, Adrienne Rich, Alice Walker, Amiri Baraka, Maxine Hong Kingston, and Wendy Rose.

Thank you to Lisa Hagan for believing in my first book, *Hive-Mind,* a memoir.

Thank you to Sara Sgarlat, my dear aunt and publicist.

Thank you to my older sister, who instilled in me the love of reading and writing.

Thank you to my dad, who taught me how to read how he reads and helped me overcome my dyslexia.

Thank you to my mom, who taught me how to stay up late reading books.

Thank you to all of my students, who teach me every day how important it is to develop our own voices and insist on life's amazing potential despite its challenges.

Gabrielle is a writer, professor, and chef. Her memoir, *Hive-Mind*, published in 2015, details her time of love, awakening, and tragic loss on an organic farm. Her first poetry book, *Too Many Seeds,* was published in 2021 by *Finishing Line Press*. Her third poetry book, *Points in the Network,* is forthcoming from *Finishing Line Press*. Her poetry has been published in the *Atlanta Review, The Evergreen Review, The Adirondack Review, San Francisco Public Press, Fourteen Hills, pacificREVIEW, Connecticut River Review, Catamaran, MacQueen's, Borderlands: Texas Poetry Review*, and is forthcoming from *The American Poetry Review*. Gabrielle is the Farm-to-Fork columnist for *Inside Sacramento* magazine. Access links to her work through her website at www.gabriellemyers.com

www.ingramcontent.com/pod-product-compliance
Lightning Source LLC
Chambersburg PA
CBHW020338170426
43200CB00006B/432